Judo

Rebecca Hunter

Photography by Chris Fairclough

W
FRANKLIN WATTS
LONDON • SYDNEY

This edition published in 2012 by
Franklin Watts
338 Euston Road
London NW1 3BH

Franklin Watts Australia
Level 17/207 Kent Street
Sydney NSW 2000

ISBN: 978 14451 0767 7

Dewey classification number: 796.815′2

A CIP catalogue record for this book is available from the British Library.

Planning and production by Discovery Books Limited
Editor: Rebecca Hunter
Designer: Ian Winton
Photography: Chris Fairclough
Consultant: Roger Houston, 6th Dan, BJA, BJA Senior Club Coach and BJA Director of Examiners

The author, packager and publisher would like to thank the following people for their participation in this book: Roger Houston and the students of the Bushido Judokwai 473 Shropshire.

Printed in China

Franklin Watts is a division of Hachette Children's Books, an Hachette UK company.
www.hachette.co.uk

Contents

Introduction to judo

Judo is an exciting combat sport that started in Japan. The word *judo* means 'gentle way'. In judo the players do not hurt each other. They use a series of throwing and grappling techniques to put their opponents on the floor and hold them there. This is how they win contests.

Judo requires agility and balance. With these skills a smaller, lighter person can overcome a larger, more powerful person.

Judo terms

A judo player is called a *judoka*. An instructor is called a *sensei*. The room or hall where judo is taught is called the *dojo*. The floor of the dojo is covered by a thick, rubber mat called a *tatami*.

The judo kit

Judo is played wearing a judo outfit called a *judogi* or *gi*. This is a thick cotton jacket and trousers. A belt is tied around the waist. Girls can wear a white T-shirt under their jacket.

Tying the belt

Hold the belt in front of you and pass the two ends around your back, returning them to your front. Now pass the left end over the right, then pull it up behind both layers of the belt. Tie the free ends together right over left and pull them tight to make a knot.

Judo grades

You can tell what grade a judoka is by the colour of their belt. Beginners wear a white belt. Advanced players wear a black belt.

Junior players have 18 grades or *mons* which progress from a red belt through yellow, orange, green and blue to brown. At each colour stage you have to learn three things and for each one you get a bar on your belt.

When you have three bars, you can move on to the next belt colour.

In the dojo

Judo is a very respectful sport. Judokas and senseis must show respect to each other at all times.

Kneeling bow

At the beginning of a session all judokas make a kneeling bow or *za-rei* to their sensei. To do this, kneel on the floor and sit back on your calves. Keep your back straight and look forward. Now bend forward and slide your hands down your thighs onto the mat. Bow your head forward but not too close to the floor.

Standing bow

All judokas make a standing bow or *tachi-rei* to each other before and after a practice, and each time they change partners.

To do this, face your partner with your hands at your sides.

Bow your head and body forwards smoothly but not too far. Hold the position for a second then stand up straight.

Safety in the dojo

In judo no-one must wear anything that could hurt anyone.

- All jewellery, watches, earrings etc must be removed.
- Long hair must be tied back.
- Fingernails and toenails must be kept short.

NEVER do judo without a sensei present. ALWAYS do what your sensei instructs immediately.

Warming up

As with all sports, it is important to warm your body up and stretch your muscles before training. This will make you perform better and reduce the chances of you injuring yourself.

Exercises

1. Shoulder rolls: Stand up straight and roll your shoulders in a backwards direction. Do ten backward rolls then ten forward.

2. Sit ups: Lie on your back with your legs slightly bent. Without moving your legs, raise your upper body into a sitting position.

3. Squats: On the floor put your hands out in front of you and stretch your legs out behind. Jump forward into a squatting position. Jump backwards and forwards several times. This will strengthen the muscles in your legs.

4. Aerobic exercises: Get warm by doing some star jumps, windmill arms or running on the spot.

Breakfalls

One of the first things you learn in judo is how to fall safely.

There are three main types of breakfall: side breakfall, back breakfall and rolling breakfall. Which one you use depends on how you are thrown.

Side breakfall

Start from a squatting position. Put your right arm out and kick your right leg forwards. Roll to the right and slap the mat with your right arm. Keep your head off the mat.

Back breakfall

Crouch in a squatting position. Extend both arms in front of you. Tuck your head in and slowly fall backwards. Slap your arms flat on the floor. The harder you slap, the easier you will land. When you have become more confident, you can try it from standing up.

Rolling breakfall

From a standing position bend and put your left hand on the mat. Tuck your head in and roll over on your arm and shoulder. As you roll on to your back, slap the floor with your right hand.

Grips and throwing

Before you can throw you need to know how to grip your partner. In a basic right-hand grip, your right hand holds the front of your partner's gi and your left hand the sleeve. Your partner will also grip you like this.

When practising judo the judoka making the throw is called *tori* and the judoka being thrown is called *uke*.

The body drop

The body drop or *tai-otoshi* is a forward throw. Tori uses a hand technique to unbalance uke.

As tori, first push uke backwards. He will resist and push forwards. Use the force of his push to pull him forwards. Then turn to the left placing your right leg across his right ankle.

Make sure that your right elbow is pushed tightly under uke's left armpit. As you straighten your leg you must lower your body pulling him off balance and onto the mat.

Forward throws

Hip throw

The hip throw or *ogoshi* uses a powerful hip movement to lift the opponent up and over.

1. Start in the basic grip position and step in front of uke with your right foot.

2. Jump round moving your right hand around uke's back. Bend your knees and pull uke's hip against your back.

3. Straighten your legs and bend forward. Pull uke over your hips and back. Release your grip on uke's right arm so that he can fall to the ground without pulling you over too.

Throws using the arms and shoulders are called *seoinage* or shoulder throws.

One-handed shoulder throw

The one-handed shoulder throw or *ippon seoinage* is a popular throw and uses a quick turn and lift.

1. Step across with your right foot and turn your back on uke.

2. Bring your right arm under uke's right arm. Push uke's arm upwards whilst holding on to her sleeve with your left hand.

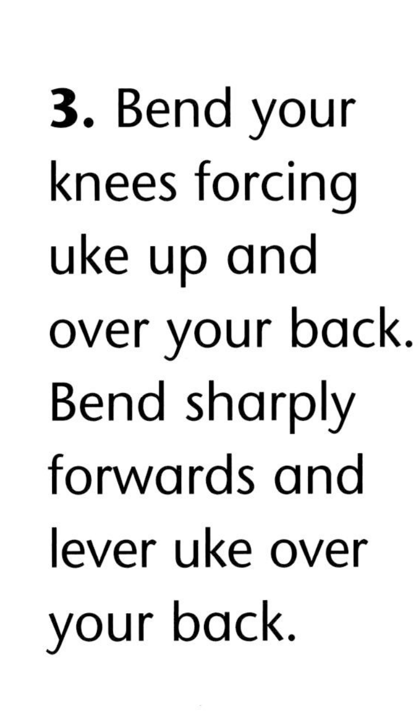

3. Bend your knees forcing uke up and over your back. Bend sharply forwards and lever uke over your back.

Foot sweeps

Throws that are used to trip your partner up with your foot are called foot sweeps.

Advanced foot sweep

In the advanced foot sweep or *deashi-barai* you force uke to take a step forwards and then sweep her foot away.

1. Push forward against uke and then step backwards to make her follow you.

2. As uke steps forward onto her right foot, sweep it away with the bottom of your left foot just as she is about to put her weight on it. At the same time pull down on uke's sleeve with your left hand.

3. Uke will lose balance and fall.

Fouls

Fouls in judo competition include: strikes to any part of the body; gouging, biting, scratching or spitting; hair pulling; bad language or loss of temper; holds where the fingers are inside the sleeve or trousers of the opponent (left) and any other unsporting behaviour. Any competitor receiving three fouls will be immediately disqualified.

Groundwork

When you and your partner have fallen or been thrown onto the mat you enter a stage called groundwork.

Groundwork is when players grapple on the mat, to get into a position where their partner cannot move. For beginners, groundwork is made up of hold-downs, which involve pinning the opponent down on the mat for up to 25 seconds.

Scarf hold

The easiest hold-down to learn is the scarf hold or *kesa-gatame*.

1. When uke has fallen at your side, quickly move and sit in the space between his right arm and his body. Hold his shoulders with both hands.

2. Wedge your hip tightly against uke's body as you put your right arm around his neck.

3. Spread your legs wide to keep stable. Lower your head and hold your opponent firmly.

Submission

When uke realizes he cannot get out of a hold-down he taps twice on the mat or on tori's body. When this happens, tori must release the hold immediately in order to avoid injury.

Judo games

Judo games are a good way for you to build up skills of balance and speed while having fun at the same time.

Sumo-style wrestling

Tie four or five judo belts together to make a ring. Two players wrestle each other inside the ring. They must try and unbalance their opponent, force them to step outside the ring or make them touch the floor with a hand or knee.

Surfing

This is a racing game. Line up several older players on their hands and knees. Smaller players stand on their backs. The pairs have to get to the other side of the mat as quickly as possible without the 'surfer' falling off. This is a good game to practise your balancing skills.

Drag racing

This is another pairs game that will strengthen your arms and legs! One player goes on their hands and knees while the other lies on their back and holds on to their partner's belt. The race is to the end of the mat.

Competitions and rules

Judo contests last for between three and five minutes depending on who is competing. The contest takes place on an 8-metre square mat with a red danger area marked around it and a green safety area outside that.

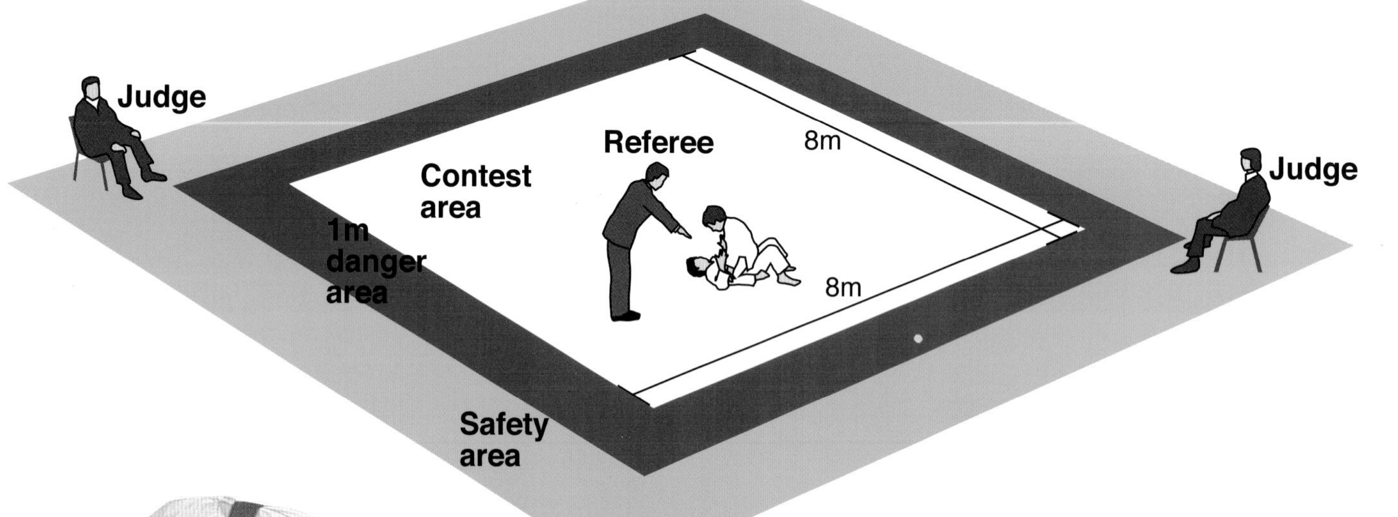

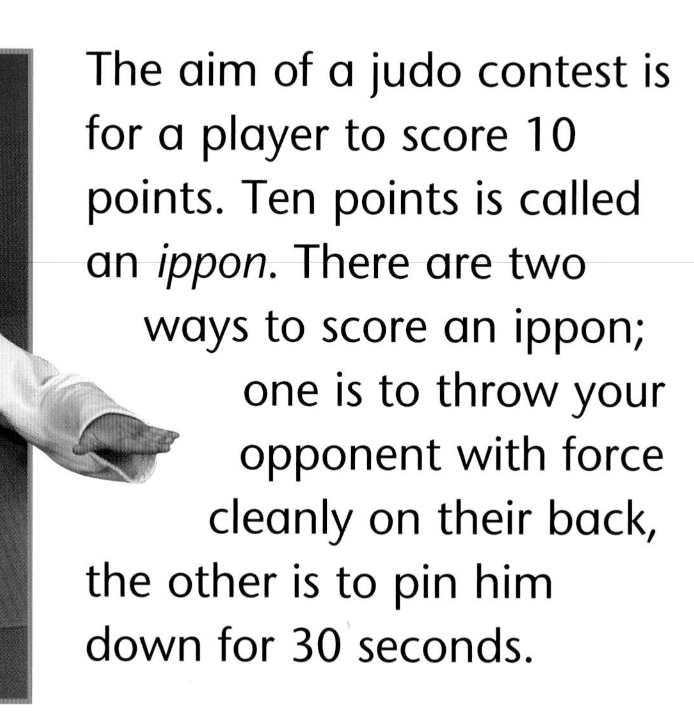

The aim of a judo contest is for a player to score 10 points. Ten points is called an *ippon*. There are two ways to score an ippon; one is to throw your opponent with force cleanly on their back, the other is to pin him down for 30 seconds.

If the throw is not quite perfect a *waza-ari* – a score of 7 points – may be awarded. Other scores for lesser throws and hold-downs are: *yuko*, 5 points, and *koka*, 3 points.

Rules

As judo is a physical combat sport, there are rules to make sure people do not get hurt.

- You cannot hold off an opponent by locking your arms out straight (below).

- You may not hold one side of your opponent's gi for more than 3 seconds without attacking them.
- You may not strike out at your opponent, kick him or push his face in any way.

Judo terms

deashi-barai advanced foot sweep

dojo the place where judo is practised

ippon a 10-point score that wins a contest

ippon seoinage one-armed shoulder throw

judo gentle way

judogi (gi) the suit worn when practising judo

judoka a judo player

kesa-gatame scarf hold

koka a 3-point score

mons junior grades

ogoshi hip throw

sensei teacher or master

seoinage shoulder throw

tachi-rei standing bow

tai-otoshi body drop

tatami judo mat

tori the person who performs a throw

uki the person who is thrown

wasa-ari a 7-point score

yuko a 5-point score

za-ei kneeling bow

Further reading

Judo in Action: Sports in Action, John Crossingham & Bobbie Kalman, Crabtree Publishing Company, 2006

Judo: A New Programme for White/Yellow Belt to Brown Belt, Hedda Sander & Bjorn Deling, Meyer & Meyer Sports Books, 2002

Judo for Juniors, Nicholas Soames, Ippon Books, 2001

Further information

British Judo Association
Suite B
Loughborough Tech Park
Epinal Way
Loughborough
LE11 3GE
Email: bja@britishjudo.org.uk
Website: www.britishjudo.org.uk

Australian Sports Commission
PO Box 176
Belconnen ACT 2616
Australia
Email: club.development@ausport.gov.au
Website: www.ausport.gov.au

Index